DINOSAUR TRACKS

LET'S-READ-AND-FIND-OUT SCIENCE®

STAGE 2

DINOSAUR TRACKS

by Kathleen Weidner Zoehfeld

illustrated by Lucia Washburn

Collins

An Imprint of HarperCollinsPublishers

Special thanks to Dr. Robert T. Bakker
for his time and expert review.

The *Let's-Read-and-Find-Out Science* book series was originated by Dr. Franklyn M. Branley, Astronomer Emeritus and former Chairman of the American Museum–Hayden Planetarium, and was formerly co-edited by him and Dr. Roma Gans, Professor Emeritus of Childhood Education, Teachers College, Columbia University. Text and illustrations for each of the books in the series are checked for accuracy by an expert in the relevant field. For more information about Let's-Read-and-Find-Out Science books, write to HarperCollins Children's Books, 195 Broadway, New York, NY 10007, or visit our website at www.letsreadandfindout.com.

Library of Congress Cataloging-in-Publication Data
Zoehfeld, Kathleen Weidner.
  Dinosaur tracks / by Kathleen Weidner Zoehfeld ; illustrated by Lucia Washburn.—1st ed.
    p.   cm. (Let's read-and-find-out science. Stage 2)
  ISBN-10: 0-06-029024-2 (trade bdg.) — ISBN-13: 978-0-06-029024-5 (trade bdg.)
  ISBN-10: 0-06-445217-4 (pbk.) — ISBN-13: 978-0-06-445217-5 (pbk.)
  1. Dinosaur tracks—Juvenile literature.   I. Washburn, Lucia.   II. Title.   III. Series.
QE861.6T72Z64 2007   2004006242
567.9—dc22

Typography by Elynn Cohen   14 15 SCP 10 9 8 7 6 5   ❖   First Edition

For Jane
—K.W.Z.

For Maia
—L.W.

Squish, squish, squish. Have you ever watched your feet making tracks in the warm sand? The beach is a great place for making footprints, and so are the muddy places at the playground after a day of rain.

All over the earth, people and animals are walking, running, hopping, and jumping. They are making tracks.

More than sixty-five million years ago—millions of years before
any people or any moose or any elephants ever lived—dinosaurs
walked the earth. They stomped through forests. They strode across
deserts. They splooshed through gloppy mud and wet sand.
Wherever they went, they left footprints behind them.

Unfortunately, most footprints get washed away by rain, waves, or floods. Or they dry out and blow away in the wind. But once in a while some tracks become fossilized.

Imagine an allosaur strolling down to a quiet stream for a drink of water. As he walks, he leaves a trail of footprints in the mud along the stream bank.

After the dinosaur has gone, the stream gently rises and spreads a layer of fine sand over his footprints.

A few years later, the tracks get buried in a layer of mud. Groundwater with carbonate dissolved in it slowly seeps through the layers. Carbonate is a type of natural cement.

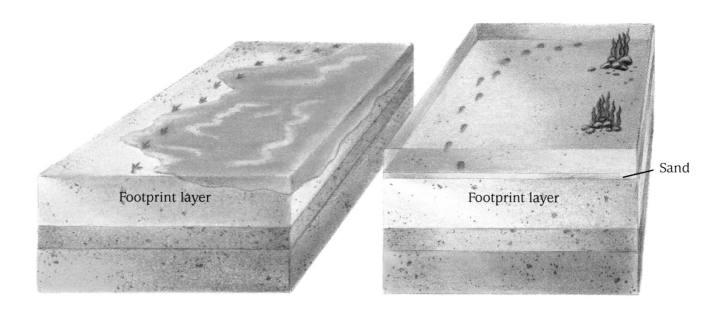

Footprint layer

Footprint layer

Sand

The cement in the mud makes it turn into solid stone. Now the dinosaur's tracks have become fossilized.

Year after year, more layers build up over the solid layer of tracks. For millions of years the fossilized tracks lie deep underground.

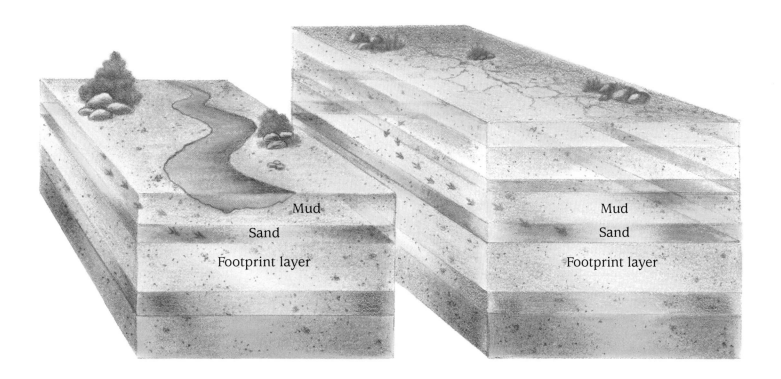

Mud

Sand

Footprint layer

Mud

Sand

Footprint layer

Then heat and pressure inside the earth begin to move the lower layers upward. At the same time, wind and rain wear away the top layers.

After millions of years underground, the dinosaur's tracks are finally out in the open again. Maybe you will be the person to find them!

If you do, you will want to tell a scientist about them. Scientists who study dinosaur tracks are called ichnologists.

Different types of dinosaurs had different kinds of feet, and they made tracks of different shapes. Ichnologists study the shapes of tracks and try to figure out which type of dinosaur made them.

From looking at fossil skeletons, we know that all meat-eating dinosaurs walked on two legs. Meat-eating dinosaurs are called theropods.

Whether they were as big as *Tyrannosaurus rex* or as small as *Coelophysis*, theropods left footprints with three main toes. Sometimes they also show the mark of a much smaller toe that pointed inward.

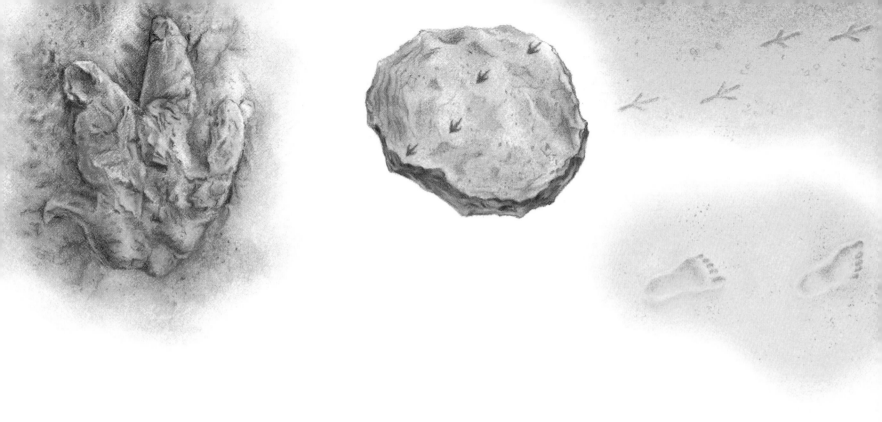

Theropod tracks look a lot like bird tracks. The tracks of most little theropods are long and narrow. Giant *T. rex*–sized meat eaters made wide tracks. You may see the mark of a blunt claw at the end of each toe print.

Plant-eating duck-billed dinosaurs and iguanodonts belong to a group called ornithopods. Like their meat-eating enemies, the theropods, most ornithopods left three-toed footprints.

But some ornithopods, such as the iguanodonts, had front paws with strong, blunt claws for walking. So they had a choice. They could walk on their big hind legs, leaving footprints with three short, stubby toes. Or they could walk on all fours, leaving little curved handprints, too.

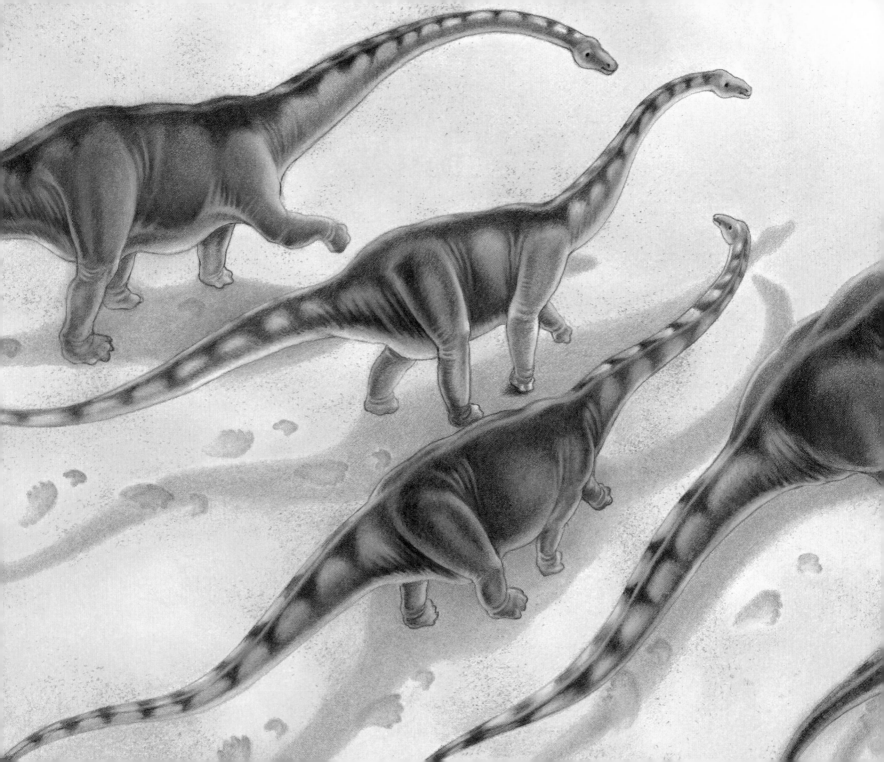

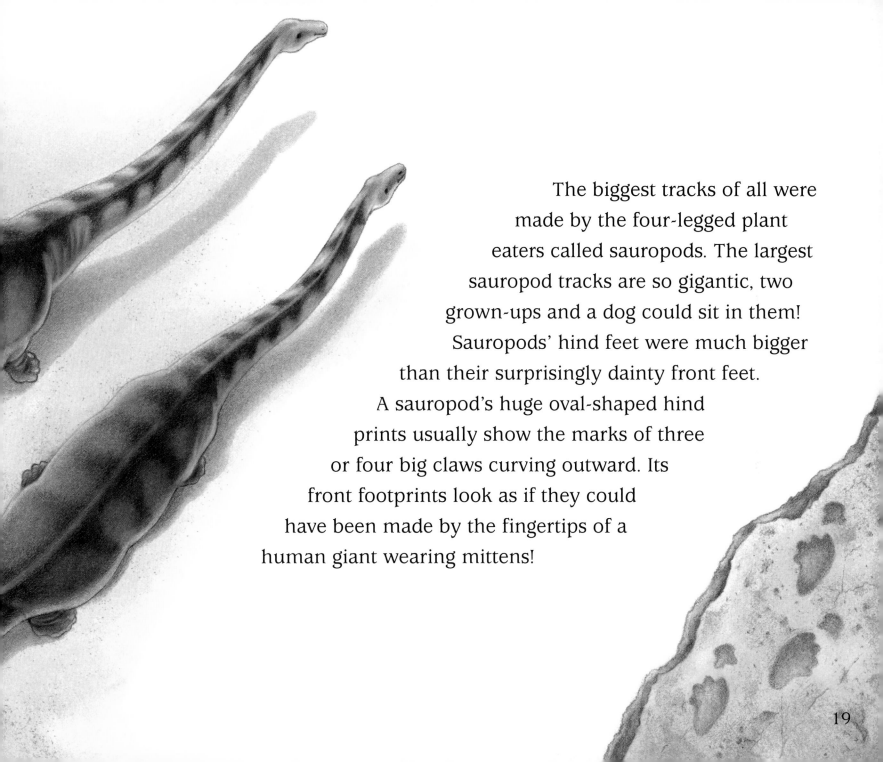

The biggest tracks of all were
made by the four-legged plant
eaters called sauropods. The largest
sauropod tracks are so gigantic, two
grown-ups and a dog could sit in them!
Sauropods' hind feet were much bigger
than their surprisingly dainty front feet.
A sauropod's huge oval-shaped hind
prints usually show the marks of three
or four big claws curving outward. Its
front footprints look as if they could
have been made by the fingertips of a
human giant wearing mittens!

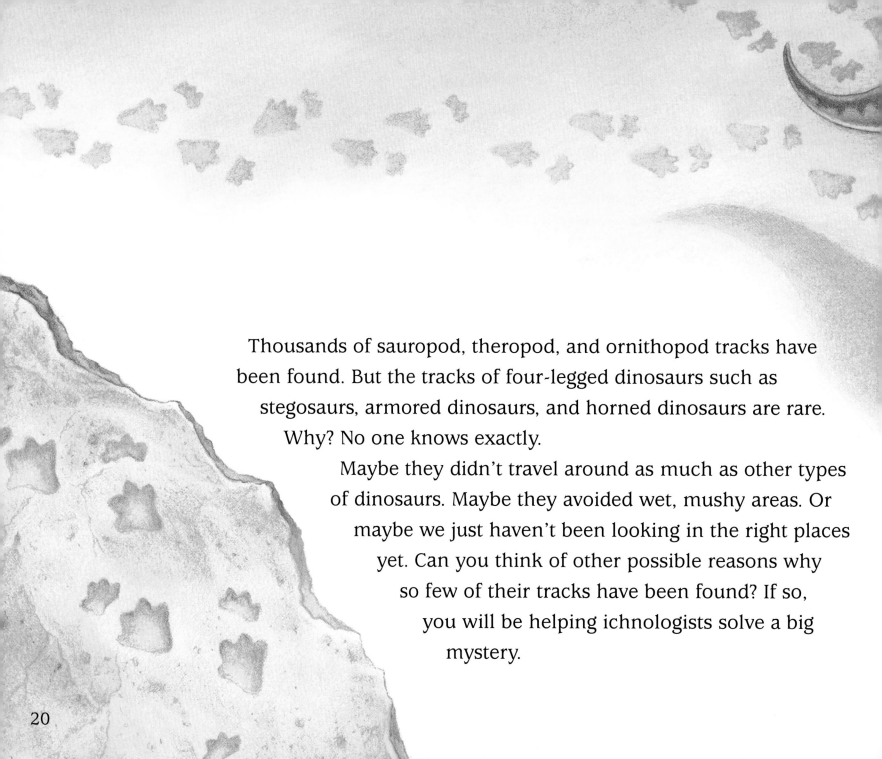

Thousands of sauropod, theropod, and ornithopod tracks have been found. But the tracks of four-legged dinosaurs such as stegosaurs, armored dinosaurs, and horned dinosaurs are rare. Why? No one knows exactly.

Maybe they didn't travel around as much as other types of dinosaurs. Maybe they avoided wet, mushy areas. Or maybe we just haven't been looking in the right places yet. Can you think of other possible reasons why so few of their tracks have been found? If so, you will be helping ichnologists solve a big mystery.

If you find a series of two or more tracks made by the same animal, you've discovered a trackway. Trackways give ichnologists clues about whether a dinosaur was walking or running.

They can show how big a dinosaur was, and if it was fast or slow. Sometimes they can even tell us about how a dinosaur lived.

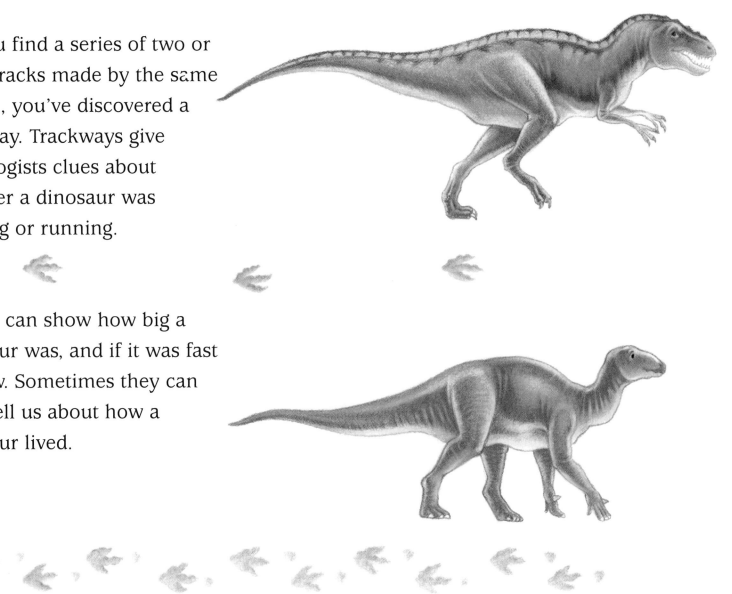

Near the town
of Bandera, Texas,
ichnologist Roland T. Bird
discovered the trackways of
at least twenty-three sauropods.
All of them were walking in the
same direction. Some of the tracks were
made by large adult sauropods and others
by half-grown sauropods and babies.

These trackways have convinced scientists that sauropods lived together in herds. In a herd, adult sauropods could have protected their young from enemies such as big, sharp-toothed theropods.

Other trackways show that ornithopods and even theropods may have lived together in groups as well.

24

The first tracks that people realized were
dinosaur tracks came from South Hadley,
Massachusetts. In 1802, a twelve-year-old farm boy
named Pliny Moody was plowing his father's field
when he struck a big slab of reddish stone. When
he lifted the slab out, he saw that it was marked with
footprints. They looked as if they had been made by
giant birds. People who saw the slab made jokes about
Moody's hefty hens. No one knew anything about
dinosaurs in 1802. It would be years before the first dinosaur
skeletons were unearthed and identified.

27

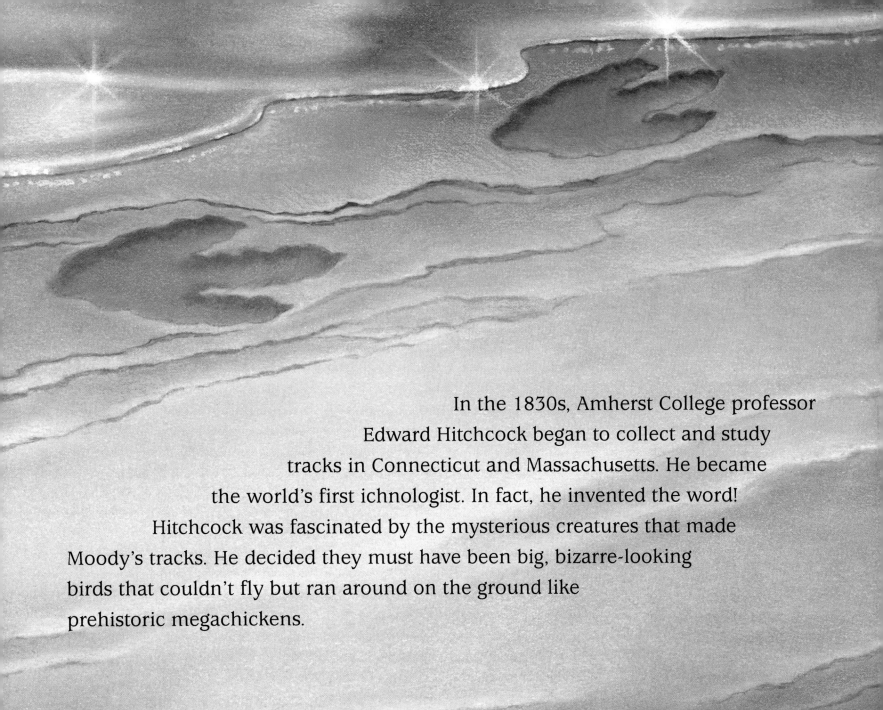

In the 1830s, Amherst College professor
Edward Hitchcock began to collect and study
tracks in Connecticut and Massachusetts. He became
the world's first ichnologist. In fact, he invented the word!
Hitchcock was fascinated by the mysterious creatures that made
Moody's tracks. He decided they must have been big, bizarre-looking
birds that couldn't fly but ran around on the ground like
prehistoric megachickens.

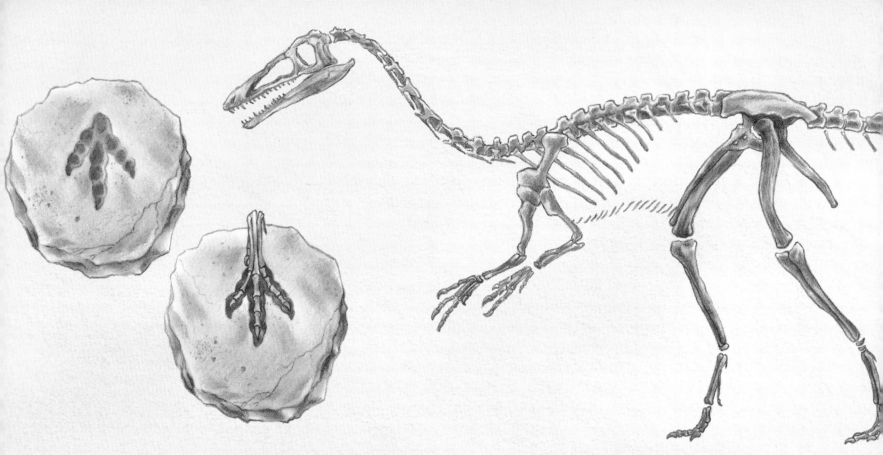

By the end of the 1800s, the first fossil dinosaur skeletons with complete sets of foot bones had been discovered. Scientists were able to compare Moody's tracks to the feet of dinosaurs. Soon it became clear—the birdlike tracks had been made by theropods.

Today we know that Hitchcock was right. In fact, dinosaurs have more in common with birds than just the shape of their feet. By comparing bird and dinosaur skeletons, scientists can tell that theropod dinosaurs were the ancestors of today's birds.

So anywhere you find areas of mud or wet sand—on the beach, or in the park or playground after a rainy day—look carefully and you may find footprints made by birds.

Squish, squish, squish.

You and the dinosaurs are making tracks!

Will some of *your* footprints ever be lucky enough to become fossilized? It could happen! But only time will tell.

31

FIND OUT MORE ABOUT FOSSIL FOOTPRINTS

If you don't have a million years to wait, you can try making fossil footprints or handprints yourself. You'll need:

Two disposable or recyclable
   aluminum cake or pie pans
   (8 to 9 inches in diameter;
   $1^{1}/_{2}$ to 2 inches deep)
Fine sand

Small pitcher of water
Epsom salt
Spoon for stirring
Small trowel

1. Fill your two cake pans with sand, about halfway to the top.
2. Pour a little water into one of the pans and mix the water and sand gently with the trowel. Make the sand just wet enough that it sticks together but isn't soupy. (Try to get the texture you'd want if you were building a sand castle!) Then smooth the surface of the sand with the trowel.
3. Put some Epsom salt into the water in your pitcher (if you have $^{1}/_{2}$ cup of water, you will want to use about $^{1}/_{4}$ cup or more of the salt). Stir until the Epsom salt has completely dissolved in the water. This is your "cementing solution."
4. Pour some cementing solution into your second pan of sand. Just as in step 2, mix thoroughly and smooth the top.
5. Then firmly press your hand or foot down on each surface of smooth, damp sand. Your prints are made!
6. Set your prints in a warm, dry place where they will not be disturbed.

7. After a few days, feel the surface of your prints. Poke the edges of your prints with your fingers. Do they feel different? Which feels more solid? Which is softer?

When mixed with water, the Epsom salt acts as a kind of glue, holding all the tiny sand grains together. Carbonates—such as calcium carbonate—found in nature act in a similar way. In nature, carbonate works to glue or cement each sand grain to all the other sand grains around it, making *sandstone.* Carbonate cements mud particles together to make *mudstone.* In places where carbonate fills up an entire layer on the bottom of a lake, it becomes *limestone.* What would you like to call the kind of stone you have made?